"What does spiritual health look like? Carl Laferton has put into our hands a simple, scriptural tool for Christians everywhere—the discipleship tool you and everyone in your church needs to grow strong in the Lord."

DANIEL DARLING. Vice President for Communications, the Ethics and Religious Liberty Commission

"The strength of the book is the accessible, interactive, concise format. Read it for yourself and give plenty of copies to your friends and family."

TIM LANE. President, Institute for Pastoral Care; author of *Living Without Worry*

"A gift to Christians. The daily pressures of life, coupled with my own sin, can make it difficult to see the work that God is doing. This is a needed tool designed to help us diagnose and treat our own spiritual health."

COURTNEY REISSIG. author of *Glory in the Ordinary* and *The Accidental Feminist*

"This is excellent. I'm going to use it with my family to contribute to their spiritual health (and mine)."

PHILIP MOORE. European Director, Acts 29

"Packed with penetrating questions and practical application, all rooted in Scripture."

NATHAN SMITH. Lead Pastor, Grace Church Bristol; Regional Leader, Sovereign Grace UK

"A brief, engaging primer for living and growing in the Christian life. Thoroughly biblical and practical, it will aid any Christian."

JASON HELOPOULOS. Associate Pastor of University Reformed Church, East Lansing, MI; author of *A Neglected Grace*

"Helpful and highly readable. Here is a gospel-hearted book that diagnoses and prescribes, offering realistic and practical encouragements for spiritual health and vitality."

NIALL LOCKHART. Minister, Ballyhenry Presbyterian Church, Newtownabbey, Northern Ireland

"How are you doing spiritually? It's a question that is vital to ask but hard to answer. So this book is a huge help. It will give you a proper reading on the pulse of your spiritual heart. It's so helpful that I'm already thinking about ways to get all the members in our church to read it!"

DAVE FURMAN. Senior Pastor, Redeemer Church of Dubai; author of *Being There: How to Love Those Who are Hurting*

"Everyone needs a check-up every now and then, and this is a terrific spiritual health-check. Here are helpfully penetrating questions and a lovely encouragement that although there are no quick steps to a thriving Christian life, we have all we need in Jesus and the means of grace."

MATT FULLER. Senior Pastor, Christ Church Mayfair, London; author of *Perfect Sinners* and *Time for Every Thing?*

"I absolutely love this! Great for getting into the habit of regular Bible-reading and prayer for the first time... or for a kick-start if things have got a bit stale. Buy it and use it— even better, buy many and use them with a friend, your family, your home group—even your whole church!"

RAMZI ADCOCK. Executive Minister, Jesmond Parish Church, Newcastle, UK

"A book that not only encourages us to greater spiritual well-being, but empowers us toward that goal."

DR FRANK SELLAR. Moderator, Presbyterian Church in Ireland, 2016-2017; Minister, Bloomfield Presbyterian Church, Belfast

CARL LAFERTON

SPIRITUAL
HEALTHCHECK

For Tom and Katie Beard.
Thanks for giving me the idea for this,
for encouraging me to write it,
and for being a great example of living it.

Spiritual healthcheck
© The Good Book Company, 2017.

Published by
The Good Book Company
Tel (UK): 0333 123 0880
Tel (North America): (1) 866 244 2165
International: +44 (0) 208 942 0880
Email (UK): info@thegoodbook.co.uk
Email (North America): info@thegoodbook.com

Websites
UK & Europe: www.thegoodbook.co.uk
North America: www.thegoodbook.com
Australia: www.thegoodbook.com.au
New Zealand: www.thegoodbook.co.nz

Unless otherwise indicated, Scripture quotations are from The Holy
Bible, New International Version, NIV Copyright © 1973, 1978,
1984, 2011 by Biblica, Inc.

ISBN: 9781784981518 | Printed in Denmark

Design by André Parker

CONTENTS

INTRODUCTION

How are you doing?

I hadn't seen my friend in a while, so it was a natural question for him to ask. And it was an easy question to answer. I talked about my job. My family. Our church. Our holiday. Everything was going fine. I was doing well. Some things were going great.

"No, I mean, how are you doing in your faith?" he said.

Oh.

I didn't know, really. I was still a Christian, which was, well, a good start. Maybe that qualified me to answer, "Fine". Perhaps it even allowed me to say "Doing well". Probably it didn't mean I could say, "Going great".

How would you answer that question? How are you doing in your Christian life? Some of us are worried when we don't need to be. Others of us are confident when we have no reason to be. Most of us know we should be growing as Christians, but aren't sure what that means exactly, or how to go about it.

You may have had a job that involved setting goals and hitting targets. It was easy to check your progress. You might enjoy gardening, where you plant and tend and enjoy the growth, or fight the weeds (or both). You may have had some kind of healthcheck, where an expert assessed you against several criteria and recommended a few changes in your diet or lifestyle in order to get healthy or stay healthy.

The Christian life is the same—we are called to make progress and grow up and stay healthy. The apostle John wrote to one of his Christian friends that he was praying "that you may enjoy good health ... just as you are progressing spiritually" (3 John v 2). And that's what this little booklet of 16 short Bible studies is about. It's a spiritual healthcheck:

- *It'll help you to diagnose your own level of Christian health—to know how you really are doing in your faith.*
- *It'll show you what vitamins God has provided you with to enable you to grow healthier and "progress spiritually".*
- *And it'll point you to the doctor whom God has provided to enable you to get on with going great in your Christian life.*

The studies first appeared as part of the *Explore* daily Bible-study series, and they proved really popular—so we thought it'd be a good idea to make them available in their own book, which is what you're reading right now.

For each study, you'll need to set aside 15-20 minutes to read, answer the questions, and think about what God is saying to you. Each day will take you into the Bible, and encourage you to apply it to yourself and respond to what God is saying by speaking to him in prayer. You can do it on your own, or with a friend, or in a group. Perhaps your whole church is working through it.

And here's what I'm praying for you. I'm praying that by the end of this spiritual healthcheck, you'll be able to answer the question, "How are you doing in your faith?"—and that the answer you'll be able to give really will be: "Going great".

1. SPIRITUALLY HEALTHY?

How are you doing in your Christian life? Really thriving... barely surviving... or somewhere in between? How can you even know how you're doing?

Welcome to your spiritual healthcheck. Over the next 16 studies, we'll move through some diagnostic questions, then identify some spiritual vitamins that will help improve your Christian health, and finish by thinking about the doctor who helps us answer the questions and enables us to self-administer the vitamins.

But first, before we get to diagnosis, we need to ask: What actually *is* a spiritually healthy Christian?

⊘ READ ROMANS 8 v 28-31

Who does God work for the good of (v 28—they are described in two ways)?

What has God decided (predestined) he will do for those people (beginning of v 29)?
Why can we be confident that this will happen (v 31)?

When I was four, I decided to be a fireman. When I was seven, I wanted to become a footballer. When I was nine, I was aiming to be a librarian. I failed in all three aspirations. When I was 19, God called me to faith in his Son, and I came to love him—and God decided that I would become like his Son, Jesus. And I may have changed my mind since I was four, seven and nine—but God will not change his mind, nor falter in his determination, nor fail in his ability, to turn me into someone who is just like Jesus, the perfect person.

So to be perfectly spiritually healthy is to be just like Christ Jesus. And to be growing more spiritually healthy is to be growing more like Christ Jesus.

Think about what Jesus was like during his time on earth. Kind. Compassionate. Courageous. Brave. Loyal. Wise. Thoughtful.

How do you feel about being like that?

⊙ READ 1 JOHN 3 v 1-2

When will we be completely conformed to the image of Christ (v 2)?

Spiritual health is being just like Christ—and, until Christ returns, you won't be in full spiritual health.

Sin-sickness will cling until the day he comes. But God is working for your good—for your Christ-likeness—in all things: the ups and the downs, the thrilling parts and the mundane parts, of normal life. None of us are completely Christ-like—but God is at work to make us more Christ-like. He is not content simply to save us through Christ; he has decided to make us like Christ.

⊘ PRAY

Adapted from John Newton:

Lord, I know I am not who I one day will be, but I thank you that I am not who I used to be. Please make me more like Christ today than I was yesterday—and please answer that prayer each day until the day I stand before him. Amen.

2. LOVE

We're going to ask five questions over five studies that help us to diagnose the state of our spiritual health, and begin to improve it. The first is: *Are you in love with Jesus?*

You might find it very helpful to ask a Christian who knows you well this question, and the next four. Their diagnosis of you may be as accurate as, or more accurate than, yours!

GOOD AND NOT-SO-GOOD

⊙ READ REVELATION 2 v 1-3

In what ways is the Ephesian church doing well, according to Jesus (speaking through his apostle John)?
If you had been a visitor to this church, what would you have made of it?

⊙ READ REVELATION 2 v 4-7

What is the problem (v 4)?

The NIV84 translates verse 4 more evocatively: "You have forsaken your first love". For all that the Ephesian church are doing, serving and enduring, there is one thing they are not doing: they are not loving Jesus.

How serious is this (v 5)?
What does Jesus promise them if they listen, change and fall in love with him all over again (v 7)?

How easy it is for churches, and Christians, to grow cold in our love for Jesus. At first, it seems so obvious and natural—we are awed and moved by our Saviour's love for us, and we respond by loving him. Then come the routines and the rotas, and without noticing, we end up doing the right things, but no longer really doing the one thing that matters—loving the One who has saved us.

And if I am struggling in the Christian life, it is likely to be rooted in a dwindling of my love for Christ.

⊙ APPLY

Do you love Jesus? Not in a sentimental, butterfly-flapping kind of way, but in a wowed, awed, moved way?
Do you love him more than you used to, or less than you used to?

HOW TO COME BACK

How can you come back to, or grow in, your love for Jesus? By seeing how he loves you. Our love is kindled as we glimpse his blazing love for us. And this is great, because we will never touch the depths or grasp the heights of his love! If you feel loveless towards Jesus, don't focus on your love for him—delight in his love for you.

⊙ READ 1 CORINTHIANS 13 v 4-7

Our love for Jesus is not like this—but his love for us is always like this. Re-read these verses, replacing "Love" and "it" with "Jesus". This is how the Lord treats you. This is how he loves you—with all your flaws and failings. Don't you love him?

⊙ PRAY

Read Ephesians 3 v 16-19 and pray for yourself what Paul prayed for his friends.

3. GRATITUDE

Here is the second diagnostic question to help you discern your true spiritual health: *Are you grateful for the cross?*

Notice the question is not, *Do you understand the cross?* Or even, *Do you tell others about the cross?* but, *Are you grateful?*

To be truly grateful for what Jesus did at Calvary, we need to begin to appreciate two truths: the truth about who we are, and the truth about what he did.

⊙ READ 1 TIMOTHY 1 v 15

What does Paul think of himself?
What does Paul know about why Jesus came?

We will not appreciate the cross until we first identify with Paul, thinking, "But in truth *I* am the worst of all sinners". Think of your thoughts of anger, lust, self-ishness and pride. Think of the things you have done that you are so relieved your nearest and dearest do not know about. These sins are not unfortunate slip-ups, committed by a basically decent person who is generally deserving of praise. They are signs of who you are—a sinner, deserving judgment.

If this makes you feel wretched, then that is a sign that the Spirit is at work in you, since one of his works is to convict us of sin (John 16 v 8-11). Paradoxcially, wretchedness is a sign of health... because it is only the wretched who can marvel at the cross (Romans 7 v 24-25); it is only the broken and humble who will be justified and exalted (Luke 18 v 14). If you think God accepts and loves you on the basis of anything you do—Bible-reading, church serving, evangelising, *anything*—then you will never be able truly to appreciate the wonder of the cross.

⊙ READ MARK 15 v 1-39 & ISAIAH 53 v 4-9

Reflect on all that Jesus went through on the first Good Friday, and as you do, repeat to yourself:

"He did that in my place, for my sake. It should have been me rejected. It should have been me punished. It should have been me forsaken. It should have been me mocked. It should have been me dying.

"But it was him. In my place, for my sake."

John Newton, the slave-trader turned pastor who famously wrote the lines "Amazing grace! How sweet the sound that saved a wretch like me", said towards the end of his life, "Although my memory is fading, I remember two things very clearly: I am a great sinner and Christ is a great Saviour". He was physically fading, but he was spiritually healthy.

⊗ PRAY

Re-read Isaiah 53 v 4-9 and pause regularly to pour out your gratitude, as a great sinner saved by a great Saviour.

⊗ APPLY

How will you make sure that you take time each day to admit your sin, reflect on the cross, and grow in gratitude?

4. EXCITEMENT

Here's the next diagnostic question: *Are you excited about the new creation?* If we are not looking forward to our next life, we will never live well in this one.

⊚ READ ROMANS 8 v 18-25

THE FUTURE

What does life appear to be like for Paul's first readers (v 18)?

How does he encourage them (v 18)?

How does creation feel about the day when Jesus returns and God's children are "revealed"—that is, their status is made utterly obvious (v 19)? Why (v 20b-22)?

It is not only believers who are waiting to be made perfect—it is the world too. Creation fell when we did, it decays as we do, and it will be restored when we are.

One reason we fail to be excited about eternity is because we've bought into cultural views of "heaven"—sitting around on a cloud in a white sheet strumming a harp is no one's idea of fulfilment. The Bible shows us something very different—an eternity spent enjoying a perfect creation, in perfect bodies, in perfect relationship with others and with God—a forever of "freedom and glory" as children of God (v 21).

THE FEELING

How should we feel about the prospect of coming home to God as his sons (v 23)?
How else should we wait for that (v 25)?

We are not to settle for the best this world offers, nor despair at the worst this world inflicts. Like a fiancée waiting for her wedding day, we wait with huge excitement; but we do wait. When we fail to remember where we are heading, we grow unexcited about our future home and half-hearted in our present obedience. We feel dissatisfied so we give in to sin, because we have forgotten that real satisfaction lies ahead of us. We feel trapped by life so we seek freedom in immorality, because we have forgotten that real freedom lies ahead of us. We experience suffering so we give in to bitterness, because we have forgotten that real glory lies ahead of us.

⊘ APPLY

How can you know you are eager about the new creation? Because your life would not make sense if there were no new creation. The "present sufferings" of Paul's readers only made sense if there was to be a "glory that will be revealed" (v 18).

Think about your life. Do you make decisions that only make sense because the new creation is ahead of you? Think about your neighbours. Do they see or hear anything different in your lifestyle and conversation that shows that you know where you are heading?

⊙ PRAY

Ask God for a greater clarity about your eternity, and a greater confidence that it is your eternity, so that you will grow more excited about eternity.

5. COMMITMENT

We're now (you're probably relieved to know!) over halfway through the diagnosis of your spiritual health. Today: *Are you committed to God's people?*

REMAINING IN CHRIST

⊙ READ JOHN 15 v 9-11. 14-15

How do we "remain in" Jesus' love (v 9-10)?
Whose joy is "complete" if we remain in Jesus' love (v 11)?
How does Jesus view those who "do what I command" (v 14-15)?

So, if you are someone who wants to grow in love for Jesus... who wants to know complete joy... who wants to be considered a friend by Jesus... who enjoys learning all that Jesus learned from his Father... then all you need to do is to "do what I command," says Jesus. And there's only one command...

THE ONE COMMAND

⊘ READ JOHN 15 v 12-13

What is the command (v 12)?
How do we know what this involves (v 12-13)?

⊘ READ ROMANS 12 v 9-16

Paul is giving the church in Rome some ways to demonstrate a love for God's people that is "sincere"—Christ-like. Here is how Christian love looks on any day when we are not called to die for our brothers or sisters.

What would each of these look like if lived out in your church?
Are there any here that particularly surprise you, or challenge you?

It is strikingly simple, and deeply challenging: our love for other believers is a Christ-given diagnostic tool for knowing if we truly love him, and are truly enjoying knowing him. It is a love that prompts and is seen in actions—honouring others, sharing with others, being hospitable to others, rejoicing and mourning alongside others.

If you do not sincerely, sacrificially, actively love God's people, then you are struggling spiritually. If you do, then you are growing spiritually. It is as simple as that.

⊙ READ 1 JOHN 4 v 9-11

If you struggle to love the other members of your church, do not look inside yourself and seek to summon up feelings of love and the will to act in love. No—look outside yourself and gaze at God's act of love in sending his Son to die for you. As you look at the cross, you will love Christ; and as you look at the cross, you will see how to love his people. After all, our King says that, "Whatever you did for one of the least of these brothers and sisters of mine, you did for me" (Matthew 25 v 40). You love him by loving his family. He loves it when you love his family.

⊙ APPLY

Look back at Romans 12 v 9-16.

How are you going to love Jesus' people this week?
How are you going to use the cross to motivate your love?

6. GODLINESS

Here, before we move on to the "vitamins", is the fifth and final question to help you assess your own spiritual health: *Are you pursuing godliness?*

POWER

> ### READ 2 PETER 1 v 1-3

Peter is writing to people who have "grace and peace", with "a faith as precious as ours" (v 1-2). He is writing to Christians.

What does God use his power to give us (v 3)?

"Godly" is an often-used, little-thought-about word. Godly means God-like—to live and think and feel in a situation just as God would.

And we know what God would do and think and feel because of our "knowledge of him who called us". We know God's glory—literally his weight, his god-ness. We know his goodness—his love and grace.

So can you live a godly, holy life? Can you defeat that sin that keeps coming back? Can you love the Christian who hurt you greatly? Yes—by his power. You can pursue godliness. But why would you want to?

PROMISES
⊙ READ 2 PETER 1 v 4-8

What else has God given us (v 4)?
What do we know we will do "through them" (v 4). In other words, what has God promised (v 4)?

One day, we will participate in the divine nature. We will not just be with God; we will be like God. We'll be back to being the people we were designed to be—people made in God's image; Genesis-1 people (enjoying being like God) rather than Genesis-3 people (grasping at being God).

What will we do if we understand this (v 5-7)?
What difference would it make to your life, and the lives of those around you, if you had each of the characteristics in verses 5-7?

Don't miss the connection between verse 4 and verses 5-7. Peter is saying, *Because you will one day be like God (v 4), on this day make an effort to become more like God (v 5-7)*. After all, it is Jesus—God on earth—who showcases all the qualities of verses 5-7 perfectly. And as we look at Jesus' self-control, perseverance, love, and so on, we see the person we'd love to be. When we see it like that, we realise that godliness is a joyful privilege more than it is a duty.

⊙ APPLY

How hard have you been pursuing godliness? How do Peter's words here motivate you to pursue it?

God's power for you means you have no reason to fail at being godly, and no excuse for failing either.

How does this most challenge you?
Think back to all five diagnostic questions. How are you encouraged? How are you humbled?

Remember, you are saved by Christ, not by your Christian life. You may need to change; but if you are trusting in Christ, then verses 3-4 are true of *you*.

7. TAKE YOUR VITAMINS

Diagnosing problems can help us start to address them—hopefully you've experienced this during the last few studies. And the Lord has also given us spiritual "health vitamins".

It's to these we now turn...

BIBLE: BAD FOR YOU?

We're joining an argument between Jesus and the Jewish religious leaders.

⊙ READ JOHN 5 v 39-40

Is the problem of these leaders that they don't read the Scriptures?

So what is their problem? What are they missing?

In Luke 24 v 32, two disciples describe the feeling of having a Bible study with Jesus: "Were not our hearts burning within us while he talked with us on the road and opened the Scriptures to us?" Is that regularly, or ever, your experience when you sit down to read the Bible?

The crucial detail here was not that the Scriptures were opened, but that Jesus was there. It is very easy to read the Bible intellectually, for more understanding; or morally, to live better; or mechanically, because we've been told that Bible-reading will help our faith. None of these ways are wrong—but on their own, they are bad for you (as they were for those religious leaders). Supremely, we need to read the Bible relationally—to meet with Jesus. Read the Bible to meet with Jesus: speak with Jesus as you read it, praise Jesus as you understand it, love Jesus more as you see his love for you—and your faith will grow stronger and your Christian life will grow healthier.

⊙ APPLY

How would you describe your approach to reading the Bible? Mainly intellectual, or moral, or mechanical, or relational?

How does this affect your faith?

⊙ PRAY

Lord Jesus, you meet with me in your word. As I read it, by the work of your Spirit, please enable me not only to understand more about you, but to know you better and love you more. Please make my Bible-reading relational. Amen.

BIBLE: AT WORK IN YOU

Vitamins work not only as we take them, but through the day. So must God's word.

⊙ READ PSALM 119 v 9-16

What words does the writer use to describe what he does with God's word?

Here is one way to enjoy Christ all day: set alarms for three points in the day. Read the Bible in the morning and take one truth about Jesus from it. When the alarm goes, pause, remember the truth, rejoice in the truth, and praise Jesus for the truth. Your enjoyment of knowing Jesus through his word does not need to—and should not—end when you close the cover of your Bible!

How are you proactively going to meditate upon Christ's ways each day?

8. LEARNING TO PRAY

Here's the second vitamin: prayer. If you struggle with prayer—if you need Jesus to "teach" you how to pray—you're in good company: so did Jesus' disciples.

WHAT WE SAY

⊙ READ LUKE 11 v 1-4

Whose interests are the focus of the first half of this prayer (v 2)?

Whose interests are the focus of the second half (v 3-4)?

How might this order shape the way we feel, and our view of our own problems, as we pray?

Given that Jesus did not pray only these words when he himself prayed (e.g. Luke 10 v 21), and given that he habitually spent hours in prayer (e.g. Mark 1 v 35), it's unlikely he wanted us to see this "Lord's Prayer" as exact wording to say, but rather, as a series of headings or topic areas.

⊙ PRAY

This week, why not structure your prayers around each clause of verses 2-4, taking one a day?

- Enjoy the truth it contains.
- Pray through the request.
- Ask for eyes to see the answers.

Why not start right now?!

WHAT WE MOST NEED

⊙ READ LUKE 11 v 5-13

What does the person in Jesus' parable want, and why (v 5-6)?

Why does he receive it (v 7-8)?

What comparison does he make between flawed ("evil") human fathers and our perfect Father in heaven (v 11-13)?

What a wonderful promise verse 10 is! We should pray with confidence. And what a wonderful invitation verse 8 is! We should pray with persistence. What a wonderful truth verse 13 is! We should pray with assurance. It's an intriguing end to the lesson— "your Father in heaven [will] give the Holy Spirit to those who ask him!" (v 13). Notice that, in prayer, we need to learn what to ask for as much as we need to learn that God is willing, and able, to answer. In the parable, the requester was making a good request for a good reason. We are to learn to ask confidently and persistently for what we most need—and supremely, what we most need is the Spirit.

This is the wonder of prayer when it matches God's priorities—God answers by giving us new experiences of the peace of the Spirit, the wisdom of the Spirit, the courage of the Spirit, the love of the Spirit, and so on. Prayer strengthens us as we re-centre ourselves on God's priorities, and as we request the work of his Spirit in our lives.

⊘ PRAY

Identify a few worries or problems in your life. Instead of asking God to take them away, work out what aspect of the Spirit's work you need to walk through them, and then ask your Father in heaven to give you the Holy Spirit.

9. HEALTH FOOD

On earth, Jesus did much of his ministry over food. And still today, he has given his church a meal that feeds us—that keeps us healthy and keeps us growing.

BAD MANNERS

⊘ READ 1 CORINTHIANS 11 v 17-22, 27-32

What is Paul criticising the Corinthian Christians for in verse 18 and verse 21-22?

Why is this serious (v 27-29)?

Receiving the Lord's Supper without "discerning the body of Christ" (v 29)—that is, without recognising that you do so as part of a church of saved sinners—means you are not eating the Lord's Supper at all (v 20). And it is so important to God that he was willing to discipline these Christians in order that they would not continue down this path towards spiritual shipwreck and eternal condemnation (v 30-32).

Why does it matter so much? Because this meal is a central means by which God strengthens his people. And such strong medicine, when misused, can be fatal.

VISIBLE WORDS

⊙ READ 1 CORINTHIANS 11 v 23-26

Notice the "For" at the start of verse 23. Here is the reason that Paul is so firm in the first paragraph of this section.

> *Who wants us to share this meal (v 23-25)?*
> *What do we remember as we eat bread and drink wine (v 24-25)?*
> *What do we look forward to (v 26)?*

The sixteenth-century Reformer John Calvin called the bread and wine "visible words". God preaches to us through the broken bread and the poured-out wine. As we re-remember the death of Christ, he moves us to appreciate more deeply how we have been brought into his family—why it is we are able to eat at his table both spiritually now and physically one day. Our eating and drinking is a public proclamation of who we are: his children, rescued by his Son's death.

⊙ READ 2 CORINTHIANS 3 v 17-18

We become more like Christ (or, to put it another way, we become healthier Christians) as the Spirit shows us Jesus—as we "see" him. We do this in his word, as we've seen. But we do this in his supper too. As the physical bread and wine enable us spiritually to "see" him on the cross, we are reminded of his love, we are moved to love him, and we are changed to be more like him. And this is why the Lord's Supper is such a wonderful means of strengthening us if we prepare for and receive it rightly—and such a dangerous thing to prepare for flippantly or receive unthinkingly.

⊙ APPLY

How is 1 Corinthians 11 v 27-29 going to help you prepare for your next sharing of the Lord's Supper?
How is verse 26 going to help you know what to think about and pray about as you receive it?

10. A HEALTHY BODY

In a sense, instead of asking, "How healthy am I, spiritually?" we should ask, "How healthy is my church, spiritually?"

That's because there are very few Christians who are thriving while their church is stagnating or struggling. God saved us to be part of his people; he placed us in a body of his people; and we each grow or shrink as spiritually as a member of his people.

That is why, in the New Testament letters, the vast majority are addressed to churches—and overwhelmingly, the content of these letters is aimed at the whole church, not individuals within the church.

PUT OFF, PUT ON

⊙ READ COLOSSIANS 3 v 5-14

What must the members of this church "put to death" by ridding themselves of it (v 5-10)?

What must God's chosen people "clothe" themselves with (v 12-14)?

A Christian who never gave into the sins of verses 5-9, and who consistently displayed the virtues of verses 12-14, would be an amazing—an extremely Christ-like—person! But notice how many of both the sins and the qualities are others-focused. Most are flaws and strengths that are displayed in community. And love, the virtue "which binds [the other virtues] all together" (v 14), is relational.

In other words, if we truly want to be spiritually healthy ourselves, we will be committed to the spiritual health of others. The maturity of other members of your church must matter as much to you as your own and the maturity of those closest to you. God has given you your church community to help you grow, as you help them grow. Paul goes on to show how we do this...

ONE ANOTHER

⊘ READ COLOSSIANS 3 v 15-17

What should rule our hearts (v 15)?

No grudges, no one-upmanship, no divisions. If Christ has made peace with someone, who are we to be in conflict with them?

What should dwell in our hearts (v 16)?
How does this happen (v 16-17)?

⊙ APPLY

Do you teach and admonish others in your church, based on what you've heard together from the Bible?

Are you someone who is willing to be taught and admonished themselves?

Why are we so often so slow to do these things for each other, do you think?

⊙ PRAY

Choose three or four people in your church. Pray that they would take off specific sins in verses 5-9 which you know they struggle with, and put on the virtues of verses 12-14. And ask for an opportunity to encourage them during the service on Sunday as you sing truths together, and after the service as you share truths together.

11. THE LORD IN CREATION

The world is set up to enable us to breathe in air that keeps us physically alive. But it is also set up so that we are able to breathe in truth that keeps us spiritually alive.

⊙ READ PSALM 19 v 1-14

The ideas of verses 7-14—that God's word refreshes us and is precious to us, and that God is our Rock and Redeemer—are fairly familiar. But the psalm doesn't start at verse 7!

What do the heavens, or skies, do all the time (v 1-2)? Since "they use no words" (v 3), in what sense do they do this, do you think?

Every single aspect of the creation points to its Creator. The intricacy of a snowflake... the power of a lightning bolt... the complexity of a cell... the beauty of a sunset. Each tells us there is a Maker, and each tells us something of the Maker. We see his glory reflected in each part of his work that we see around us.

To what does David compare the sun (v 4b-6)?

In the Old Testament, God describes himself as a bridegroom, with his people as his bride (e.g. Hosea 2 v 14-23) The Gospels record Jesus using that bridegroom imagery for himself (Mark 2 v 18-20). And Revelation reveals that when the Lamb, Jesus, returns, it will be to hold a wedding feast for his bride, the church (Revelation 19 v 7-9), ushering us into a restored world where there will be no need for a sun, "for the glory of God gives it light, and the Lamb is its lamp" (21 v 23).

So when David describes the sun as "a bridegroom" (Psalm 19 v 5) that gives warmth to all (v 6), he is not just clutching at any old simile. He is saying, *The sun reminds me of you, God—reminds me of your power, your love, your warmth*. And, living after Jesus died to rescue his bride, we can say, *The sun reminds me of you, Jesus—of your power, love and warmth, and of your return, when you will be all the light we need*.

The triune God has painted himself into his creation masterpiece. He made lightning to remind us of the sudden, powerful return of Christ (Luke 17 v 24) He made snow to show us what he does with our sin (Isaiah 1 v 18). He made fire to tell us about the power of his purity and the warmth of his Spirit (Exodus 19 v 18; Acts 2 v 1-4). He made rocks to enable us to understand his stability (Psalm 19 v 14). Everywhere in his creation, he is showing us himself.

Remember, spiritual health means becoming more and more like Christ (Romans 8 v 28-30). We become more and more like Christ as we see more of Christ (2 Corinthians 3 v 18). And we see Christ throughout his creation, as we learn to look at it with eyes ready to see it "declare the glory of God" (Psalm 19 v 1).

⊘ APPLY

As you go about your day, look for God—Father, Son, and Spirit—in his creation. Ask him to point you to himself—who he is and what he's done—in what you see, so you might appreciate and enjoy him all day.

12. THE GIFT OF SUFFERING

A healthy Christian is not necessarily a healthy person. A hard truth to grasp is that your suffering is a divine gift to keep you trusting and keep you healthy (spiritually).

GENUINE FAITH

⊙ READ 1 PETER 1 v 3-7

Because Jesus rose (v 3), what can his people look forward to (v 4)?

How do we know we'll get there (v 5)?

With what emotion should we respond to this (beginning of v 6)?

But what are Peter's readers going through (v 6)?

Why have "these ... come" (v 7)?

Suffering shows what, or who, we really trust in... and what, or who, we find our joy in. Suffering hurts because it involves the removal of a happy circumstance (e.g. a relationship, or a career, or good health, or a secure home). But for the Christian, it does not involve the removal of our joy—because our joy was never primarily found in that thing, but in Christ and our eternal home with him. And so suffering proves the "genuineness of your faith"—not to God (he already knows!) but to you. When we are at our weakest but we cling on to Christ, we can see that our faith is not fake, but real.

⊙ APPLY

Have you ever experienced a time when you were suffering greatly, and saw that your faith was genuine and your joy was not extinguished? How does that encourage you?

Are you suffering right now? How might God be using this suffering to:

- *show you your faith is genuine?*
- *enable you to locate your joy each day in him, not in circumstances?*
- *make you more like Jesus?*

RUN TO GOD

In all the Bible, Job is the human whose suffering we see in most detail, and whose response we see at most length. By Job 2 v 8, Job has lost his wealth, his children, his house and his health—and he has no idea why.

⊘ READ JOB 2 v 9-10

What does Job's wife tell him to do? Why is this understandable?

I have not suffered as Job and his wife did. But I have heard my own mind recommending what Job's wife did.

How does Job respond (v 10)?

In suffering, we either run away from God in despair and bitterness, or towards God in desperate trust. The first is easier; the second is greater. It assures us of our faith and of our future, and means that we can be joyful, not crushed.

⊘ PRAY

How do you need to pray for yourself in light of these truths?
Who else do you need to pray for?

13. THE FAMILY DOCTOR

It is one thing to see where we are struggling, and the ways God has provided us with to keep growing in our faith. It is quite another thing to actually change.

In fact, it is impossible for us to do that. Which is why it is wonderful that God has given us someone to enable us to make those changes. And that person is... himself: his Spirit.

If you want to be a healthy, thriving Christian, you will need to put effort in (2 Peter 1 v 5, 10). But you will need to make that effort while relying on God's Spirit to take that effort and use it to change you. To put it another way, the Spirit is the doctor who applies the God-given vitamins to our spiritual lives. We're going to take three studies to see how the Spirit is working in you.

BIRTH

⊙ READ JOHN 3 v 3-8

How does someone become part of God's kingdom, en-joying new life (v 3, 5-6)?

The Spirit is the midwife of our eternal lives. Without his work, you would not be a follower of Jesus. "No one can say, 'Jesus is Lord,' except by the Holy Spirit" (1 Corinthians 12 v 3).

FAMILY

⊙ READ ROMANS 8 v 10-17

If we have the Spirit (that is, if we know Jesus as our Lord)...
- *what can we look forward to (v 11)?*
- *what will we seek to do (v 12-13)?*
- *who are we (v 14)?*
What are the implications of having been "born again" into God's family (v 15-17)?

Part of the Spirit's work in God's people is to assure them of who they are, enable them to experience the joy of who they are, and help them to live as who they are. The more confident we are that we "are the chil-dren of God ... heirs of God and co-heirs with Christ" (v 14, 17), the more we will enjoy that status and the intimacy with our Creator God that it brings (v 15). And the more we enjoy being children of God, the more we'll want to "put to death the misdeeds of the body" (v 13), which is our obligation to our new Father and our new family. And even as we seek to do this, we find that it is "by the Spirit" that we are enabled to do it (v 13).

⊙ APPLY

Do you struggle for assurance of your status? Will you ask the Spirit daily to remind you that you are a child of God?

Do you struggle for enjoyment of your status? How will you "cry 'Abba, Father'" and how will you remind yourself of your glorious inheritance?

Do you struggle to live out your status? What "misdeeds of the body" do you need to ask the Spirit to enable you to stop playing with, and instead put to death?

14. THE GROWER OF FRUIT

Letting the Spirit do his work in us is not easy—because in a very real sense, we don't want him to do it.

⊙ READ GALATIANS 5 v 15-26

THE BATTLE

What does Paul say will not happen if and as we "live by the Spirit" (v 16)?

The "flesh" is our "sinful nature" (NIV84)—our old selves, which were ruled by sin.

What is the relationship between the Spirit living in us and our old selves clinging to us (v 17)?

If you feel that living as a Christian is a constant battle within, be reassured—that's what truly living as a Christian involves! It's only if we feel there is no battle that we should be concerned, because that means our flesh is winning.

How do verses 18 and 25 tell us what it means to "live by the Spirit"?

In verse 18, Paul is contrasting two motivations for obeying God—the Spirit and being "under the law". The Spirit motivates us by reminding us of our Spirit-given identity—children of God (Romans 8). Living "under the law" means we are driven by earning our identity—so we're motivated by pride (because we're better than others) or fear (because we're terrified God might reject us). So living "under the law" can therefore never produce fruit such as peace or lack of conceit and envy (v 22, 26).

THE GROWTH

Which "acts of the flesh" (v 19-21) are you battling against, or being defeated by?
Which parts of the "fruit of the Spirit" (v 22-23) do you see growing in your life? Which feel most distant from you?

Verse 24 reminds us of what has happened to our old, sinful selves—our "flesh": it has been crucified. When Christ died, it died—the penalty for it was taken and its power over us was broken. But its pull remains—so we need to keep killing what has been crucified. And we do this by keeping "in step with the Spirit" (v 25). He strengthens us to say "no" to our flesh, and as we do this, he grows in us his fruit. Our job is to let the Spirit do his job.

⊙ PRAY

Identify the acts of the flesh you most struggle with, and ask the Spirit to help you want to live as a child of God when you feel that tug.

Identify the parts of the fruit of the Spirit that you most struggle to grow, and commit to working with the Spirit to enable those virtues to grow in you.

Finally, pray for your church. The "you" in these verses is plural—you will crucify the flesh and grow this fruit as part of your church. So pray these things for your church, as well as for yourself.

15. THE GIVER OF GIFTS

Healthy Christians are serving Christians, because the Spirit works in us to work through us to help God's people.

GOD'S GIFTS

⊘ READ 1 CORINTHIANS 12 v 1-11

Why are you good at particular things (v 4-6)?

For what purpose are you good at those things (v 7)?

The list in verses 8-11 is not an exhaustive list of gifts of the Spirit. Paul intends to give a flavour of the gifts, so that we begin to see that they come in a great variety, but come from one source (v 11), and for one purpose—the common good of God's people (v 7).

⊙ APPLY

Your talents are not from you, and your talents are not for you.

Does this truth mean you need to change your view of your abilities in any way?

Is there anything you need to speak to a church leader about, e.g. offering your services to your church?

CHURCH BODY

⊙ READ 1 CORINTHIANS 12 v 12-31

Paul is using the image of a body to describe your local church—and your part in it.

What point is he making about your place in your church in:
- *v 15-20?*
- *v 21-25?*
- *v 26?*

⊙ PRAY

Ask God, by his Spirit, to give you a right view of yourself and your church—neither thinking you have nothing to offer others, nor that you have no need of others. Ask for such an identification with your church that you suffer when another member does, and feel joy when another is honoured.

THE MOST EXCELLENT WAY

⊙ READ 1 CORINTHIANS 13 v 1-7

What kind of very godly-looking actions are potentially useless (v 1-3)? Why?

Why does this mean you could apply chapter 12 perfectly, and uselessly?

Part of my problem when it comes to my spiritual health is this: *I just don't love others very much.* That's why I use my Spirit-given gifts in my time, for my own sake; or only use them for others in a grudging, is-this-enough-now way or a proud, I-hope-people-notice way. Maybe you're similar. Thankfully, as we've seen, we don't have to look inside ourselves to summon up the kind of love Paul describes in verses 4-7. We look to God. We look to the Father, who out of love sent his Son; to the Son, who out of love went to the cross; and to the Spirit, who grows his fruit in us—the first part of which is... love (Galatians 5 v 22).

A healthy Christian is a serving Christian and a loving Christian. And that is what the Spirit is working to make you.

16. HEALTHY LIVING

The last session in our spiritual healthcheck gives you an opportunity to look back with reflection, and look forward with decision.

DO NOT MERELY LISTEN

⊘ READ JAMES 1 v 22-25

What does God's law offer us (v 25)?

How does this motivate us not to make the mistake described in verses 22-24?

Reading God's word never leaves us unchanged. It either results in us "doing it" and enjoying the freedom of living the way we were designed to, under God's law—or it leaves us deceiving ourselves, because we think that reading is what counts. It isn't. *Doing* is.

The word brings us to Christ, shows us Christ, and then tells us to live like Christ. So this series is only helpful for your spiritual health if it results in you doing what the word has been prompting you to do!

⊘ APPLY

Let's return to the diagnosis stage. How did you measure your spiritual health on these five yardsticks?

- *Are you in love with Jesus?*
- *Are you grateful for the cross?*
- *Are you excited about the new creation?*
- *Are you committed to God's people?*
- *Are you pursuing growth in godliness?*
- *How might you address ways in which you have stagnated? How will you ensure that you are praying about them?*

Now let's look at the vitamins. How has this series helped you to make best use of:

- *Bible-reading?*
- *prayer?*
- *the Lord's Supper?*
- *your church community?*
- *creation?*
- *suffering?*
- *Are there any practical changes you need to make to ensure a "healthy diet"?*

Lastly, let's reflect on the way the Spirit, our doctor, administers the treatment we need.

How have you been encouraged and challenged to rely on and work alongside the Spirit as he works in you?

TRANSFORMED

⊙ READ ROMANS 8 v 28-30 & 2 CORINTHIANS 3 v 17-18

Above all, remember what spiritual health looks like— it looks like Jesus. The healthy Christian is the Christlike Christian. One day, you will be perfectly like him; today, you can grow more like him. And you do that as you see him, as the Spirit shows you Christ in his word and prayer, in his supper, in his people, in his creation and through the circumstances he sends you.

⊙ PRAY

Reflect on how you have been excited about and moved by Christ. Thank God for him. Ask him, by his Spirit, to keep showing you Jesus, and where you are not like Jesus, so that you keep changing to be like Jesus.

HELP TO STAY HEALTHY...

Explore Daily Bible Devotionals help you open up the Scriptures to enjoy meeting Jesus there. Published as a quarterly booklet, *Explore* is also available as an app, and features Christ-centred insights from pastors such as Timothy Keller, Mark Dever, Christopher Ash, Tim Chester and Sam Allberry.

thegoodbook.co.uk/explore
thegoodbook.com/explore

BEST RESOURCE 2017

We all want to pray and know it's important, but our prayer lives can get stuck in a rut.

These **5 Things to Pray** books will give you lots of ideas when you don't know what to pray. Each page takes a passage of Scripture and suggests five things to pray for a particular person or situation. When we pray in line with God's priorities as found in his word, our prayers are powerful—they really change things.

KEEP ON GROWING

Enjoy thinking more about what Christian growth is, and how we can get out of a rut and beyond our routines to enjoy thriving in our Christian lives. Lots of the themes in *Spiritual Healthcheck* came from this readable, practical, Christ-centred book!

"Honest and oh-so-encouraging, this book should be on every church bookstall and in every Christian's hands."

MICHAEL REEVES, Director of Union; author of *Rejoicing in Christ*

the good book
COMPANY

BIBLICAL | RELEVANT | ACCESSIBLE

At The Good Book Company, we are dedicated to helping Christians and local churches grow. We believe that God's growth process .always starts with hearing clearly what he has said to us through his timeless word—the Bible.

Ever since we opened our doors in 1991, we have been striving to produce resources that honour God in the way the Bible is used. We have grown to become an international provider of user-friendly resources to the Christian community, with believers of all backgrounds and denominations using our Bible studies, books, evangelistic resources, DVD-based courses and training events.

We want to equip ordinary Christians to live for Christ day by day, and churches to grow in their knowledge of God, their love for one another, and the effectiveness of their outreach.

Call us for a discussion of your needs or visit one of our local websites for more information on the resources and services we provide.

Your friends at The Good Book Company

UK & EUROPE   thegoodbook.co.uk   📞 0333 123 0880
NORTH AMERICA   thegoodbook.com   866 244 2165
AUSTRALIA   thegoodbook.com.au   (02) 9564 3555
NEW ZEALAND   thegoodbook.co.nz   (+64) 3 343 2463

 WWW.CHRISTIANITYEXPLORED.ORG
Our partner site is a great place for those exploring the Christian faith, with a clear explanation of the good news, powerful testimonies and answers to difficult questions.